THRESHOLD

THRESHOLD

New and Selected Poems

Cary Waterman

NODIN PRESS

First Thaw was originally published by the Minnesota Writers' Publishing House in 1975. *The Salamander Migration and Other Poems* was originally published by the University of Pittsburgh Press in 1980. *Dark Lights the Tiger's Tail* was originally published by Scopcraeft Press in 1981. *When I Looked Back You Were Gone* was originally published by Holy Cow! Press in 1992. *Book of Fire* was originally published by Nodin Press in 2011.

The author wishes to thank the following journals and collections in which the poems in *First Thaw, The Salamander Migration and Other Poems, Dark Lights the Tiger's Tail, When I Looked Back You Were Gone* and *Book of Fire* first appeared, some in slightly different versions: *American Poetry Review, Blue Earth Review, Common Ground Review, Connecticut River Review, Cutthroat, Dacotah Territory, The Decade Dance, Dust and Fire, Great River Review, Green Mountain Review, Labyris, The Literary Review, The Louisville Review, Milkweed Chronicle, Minnetonka Review, 25 Minnesota Poets, Minnesota Times, Moons and Lion Tails, New Guard Review, New Jersey Poetry Journal, Nimrod, North Country Anvil, Northeast, Northeast Journal, Painted Bride Quarterly, Poets On: Loving, Primavera, Poets Against the War, Poetry Now, Preview, Rag Mag, Room of One's Own* (Canada), *The Roundtable, Sing Heavenly Muse, Steelhead, South Dakota Review, Tendril, This Sporting Life, The Webster Review, Turtle Quarterly, Water~Stone, Westend, What Light, Wooster Review,* and *Yarrow.*

Grateful acknowledgement is made to the following publications where the following new poems or previous versions of them first appeared: *I-70*: "Noah's Wife"; *Miramar*: "September Gold"; *Poetry Quarterly*: "Landing Planes"; *Water~Stone*: "The Cells-The Moon"; *Poetry City, USA*: "This Is Not a Poem"

"Leaving: Cleaving" won second prize in the Federico Garcia Lorca Poetry Contest and was published in *Green Briar Review.* "Lluvia" won second prize and was published in the *Common Ground Review.*

Cover painting by Patricia Canelake from the series *Leashed/Unleashed*

ISBN: 978-1-947237-10-0

Library of Congress control number: 2018946887

Nodin Press
2514 Cedar Lake Road
Minneapolis, MN 55416
www.nodinpress.com

For all those who have walked with me

CONTENTS

from *First Thaw* (1975)

from *The Salamander Migration* (1980)

from *Dark Lights the Tiger's Tail* (1981)

from *When I Looked Back You Were Gone* (1992)

from *Book of Fire* (2011)

New Poems (2018)

I.

II.

III.

What would rescue her was time itself, and above all, its inexorability, the utter impossibility of anything ever staying the same.

– Francine Prose
"Hansel and Gretel"

from

FIRST THAW

(1975)

DOMESTICATION

Tonight
a voice rises like an arrow
from the woods,
half female,
half something else.

An owl maybe
with a furred body pierced
on short forked fingers.

Inside the kitchen
the cat who is female
turns from her instinct to prowl
and keeps within the secure circle of light.
And so do I.

Outside
the dark buzzes
at the window.

PLAYING WITH WATER

for Devin

Your mother is in the tub
trying to wash herself away.
She is a whale in the water,
tail and rib.
Nothing fits.

You are at the sink.
You have a cardboard strip
that the water runs up and down.
You have discovered the aqueduct.

You turn, dip your hand
in my water and I roll
in this high-sided casket
with the way your hand
directs the current.

You talk to me by sonar.
I echo back,
tell you what I remember
of birth.
You pat my grey head, put
a long red flower in my mouth.
I eat it,
take the white towel,
step onto the shore.

HUSBANDRY

The ducks are obedient.
Every night they anticipate like wives
going to bed in their wooden box,
protection against coon and skunk.
My son says they wear pajamas.
I know better.
I know they fear the eyes
that come through the dark,
eyes that slip under their fence like water,
swim the small pool,
strike onto the land with a fist.

They will survive.
They have become pets
and like a mirror they are docile,
printed with the image that feeds them.
They will get fat because they are confined
and lay eggs and keep them warm.
And when the flock is hatched
they will mark off the days
until the first Thanksgiving.

AFTER THE PIG BUTCHERING

What does the pig think of the dawn?
They do not sing but they hold it up.

— Pablo Neruda

I go back two days later
for the skin.
It is dismal weather
The floor of the shed is wet
where blood mingles with red paint
and the dark soft manure.
It is a watercolor of confusion and pain,
of the loss of thought.
Feeding pans are in chaos,
tipped like crazy men into corners.

I have gone back to pick up the skin.
We left the entrails to droop in the compost heap.
I see them sinking like heat into the ground.
I know parts of them are ovaries.
And there are two blue-lipped stomachs
that seem to smile.
The skin is on the roof of the shed.

Carrying it I can tell that it weighs
about as much as my three-year old son.
It is solid like a head against my breasts.
I like carrying it and squeeze it closer,
rub my cheek into it.
The taut nipples are watchtowers
on both sides of the river we cut open.
I am bringing it home.

Now the smell is on me,
grease on my hands.
I bring it all into the house.
It slides around the doors,
under the beds.
It is pungent,
obsessive.

FIRST THAW

for Bridgit

By noon winter is already dead
and fog drapes Le Sueur County
like a congregation of ghosts.
They hold hands around tree trunks.
They hide in their winding sheets
what my eyes need to see.

We lose our balance in this weather,
squint to tell earth from air,
and reach for familiar things –
a tree or the smell of an animal to steady us.

All day my daughter said there were voices singing.
They made her feel possessed.
Like the voices of the womb
they danced against each other singing –

> *Come –*
> *Spring runs off the hills like a madwoman.*
> *Don't wait.*

LEARNING THE NAMES

I have come to the place where birch
and aspen grow all the way
down to the water.
My canoe slips between them,
a silver fin spreading the lips
of the Ottertail River.

Ruffled grouse drum in reeds.
Where I drift I am close to the nests
of red-winged blackbirds.

These names become the guide.
They mean a place between, a passage.
They cry across the water defining
the heavy forest I have come from.

Now there are loons walking on the water.
They dive and come together.
Making love they beat each other
with dark and tensile wings.

VESPERS

We sleep most of the afternoon
finally lifting up into the hot bowl
of five o'clock.
We pull the shades,
fit them stiff over the mouth
of windows,
over the flies caught there
vertical against light.
The difficult life of almost everything
curls into a smile at our front door.

This is the time of day
water hysterically laughs itself
into the sink.
Plates on the table fidget
nervous between knives and forks.
In the distance of this waking
you slip from me,
a blade from my fingers,
hand at the back of my head.
Together we wait for night,
for blue light,
the cinnamon taste of dark.

JUNE POEM IN FAVOR OF NOTHING

Pale like a winter radish
I slide with my long green chair
into the trees and gooseberry bushes.
When my book bores me
I listen to the birds.
They tell me their predictions for July and August.
I move along graciously until the creek breaks open
with buffalo-head carp slapping their way
back to the lake after last night's storm.
There are dozens propelling themselves upstream
like children's tin toys,
their pink bellies graveling on sand.

You come and we wade in together,
me with a great silver shovel,
you with your green pitchfork.
Now they are all over our bare feet,
confused and tired and full of eggs.
I want to hold the biggest one,
smooth her scaled skin.
You pitchfork three in the belly
and tell me I haven't done a thing all day.
I wade out into mud.
It is warm. It invites me to sink.
I think about putting up my hammock,
learning how to draw.

DEATH ON THE FARM

Halfway between the house and the barn
there's a dead Holstein dairy cow,
black and white like a map of the world.
She is big-eared, square-toothed
and frozen solid.

Whoever said death was fluid
and wore long garments like a wind?
Death is a pile.
The truck from the rendering kitchen
should have been here days ago.
Now it is too late.
The cow is beginning to come back to life.
I can see her breathing from the window.

She looks comfortable there
even though dogs have begun chewing
a dark hole that will end at her heart.
After they come to take her,
after her fingered milk bag,
her white braced hips are gone,
her breathing will go on in that place,
up and down against the weeds,
in and out filling the dark space
that goes between us
when we are not looking.

PIG POEM

The pig's ears blossom and fold
like lush jungle lilies.
It is their only attractive feature
except for their shell-shaped feet
that try to escape each night.

Each pig roots under the prickly ash,
undermines the shed's foundation,
eats the red impatiens, and
buries clothes left lying around.
They are the fat of existence,
a greasy black skillet.

The Dani of New Guinea have lived forever
on pigs and sweet potatoes.
They have never been Christianized.

from

THE SALAMANDER MIGRATION

(1980)

ME, LEARNING TO DANCE

I don't know how.
And so you pose before me –
a right angle,
a cock-eyed telephone pole
ready to begin.

Mother watches, approving.
She is tiny.
I am tiny.
And you are so much bigger
weaving like Goliath
in the space before me.

Then we start this strangeness
bobbing and heaving like heavy ducks,
right, left,
right, right, left,
you going one way,
me following like an afterthought.
Steam swirls from my head
as we circle the room
minutes before my date arrives.

But it is too late.
Here he is with a corsage box,
two pink tea roses squeezed
by gregarious carnations.
I go off with him
into the night.
But I do not love him.
It is you I love
but I will never tell you,
never tell you,
never.

AFTER A DEATH

You have planted Irish heather
purple by the rocks.
And funkia, the green and white plant
for poor soil, wetness,
and sunlessness.
And you have cultivated also
the sexual holly,
stiff leaves glossy
with love.

You tell me how my father
would count the trees
as he walked his lot in evening,
counting maple, pine,
and sassafras, the mitten-leaved tree.
He would stop before the huge elm
rotting at the boundary line
and dominating everything,
its roots reaching toward
the house foundation.

You will have it cut down,
the massive trunk,
the branches filled with words of disease
hanging over the porch, garage,
your new flower bed.
You will drive out the black ants
who have gathered there in families
and who are making longer
and longer explorations
leaving odor trails all the way
to the back door of this house.

VISITING THE CEMETERY

The bodies of immigrants
settle for the last time
in official rows.
It is as crowded here
as it was in steerage,
the Irish and Germans
untranslatable
in the single language
of death.

There are few who come to see
the ocean of tombstones,
the stone trees,
the stone-colored pigeons
picking through summer grass.

My family lies in
narrow beds,
the beautiful women,
Lizzie, Rose, Bridgit,
all braided and promised.
Their husbands lie beside them,
Peter, John, and Charles,
my grandfather who traded
a German village for washing floors
in the city hospital,
for the dull slosh of the mop,
never saying how much it cost him.

MORNING

In the morning
a yellow slap of light
reaches around the clouds.

I am awake.
I want something good to hold me
like the silken strings
on the sky diver's
parachute.

Instead I continue
to fall down into the day,
away from dream
and faithfulness to dark.
The day reaches through me
for voices and food.

Wait.
I hear its mouth
slip over the doorknob,
its fist begin to knock.

ELDERBERRY JAM

You have been gone hours
foraging in the woods
behind our house.
In your absence
the night came and stood
at the back door.

Now you come back,
stand in the doorway,
your hair wet with dew.
In your hand a
brown bag in which
the elderberries are captive,
still rigid,
still resisting on
their hooks of stem.

After we clean them
I start the jam.
In an old pot
the berries burst into purple.
They are little skulls of stain.
I add sugar,
that white iceberg,
and a scant touch of water
to start the boil.
Now the fruit is becoming tender,
the juice begins to flow.

At the moment of mashing
they rise up shaking fists,
boiling and turning
like hot rock

and push to the center,
to smother,
to go down in the purple
face of the pot.

And the night –
how it comes into the kitchen,
surrounds us,
pouring down through
the rusty screens.

HARVESTING

This is the silence of full spaces.
Time and the fall conspire against us.
There is sadness in the harvested fruit,
sadness in all the children sitting
at the silence of heavy desks.

Sometimes I do not know what we do.
Sometimes I do not know where
the sadness comes from
and for what purpose.

But tonight I will prepare a stew.
I will pick the longest carrots
drunk on their own fulfillment.
I will pick a finale of onions,
a wheelbarrow of potatoes.

We will sit down together.
We will begin again,
all of us,
all over again.

GETTING OLD

You take pills,
have coughing fits at dark.
I have two ocean currents
deepening around my mouth.
Our children look at us secretly.
They know we cannot tell anymore
what they are thinking.

In the marriage blender
we have been set on chip.
Pieces fell away,
dried like snipped ends of beans.

Things continue to fall from us –
skin,
children,
ambitions.
They transform themselves
to a life on their own,
forgetful,
mute.

THE FRONT LINES

I cross my arms,
let my hands swim up
like spawning salmon
insides the sleeves of my sweater.

The rest of my body
might suffer.
The head with its infinite
calculations.
And the thoughtless feet.
Even the belly although
it is the softest
and most hidden.
But the suffering of hands
would mean the end of love,
a shriveling of light.

If I hold my hands to my face
certain empty afternoons
I see the network again,
the lives like fossils in amber
pressed into my palms.
The crosshatch of the life line.
The tributaries of love.

Looking into my hands I see
that it is spring, raining.
The roads are rutted with mud.
Heavy guns and high-wheeled carts
filled with wounded go
single file, creaking.
They all lead south,
all coming back from the front lines
of a war fought in winter
in which many others have died.

A LIGHT IN THE DOORWAY

Anything approaching us we try to understand, say
Like a lamp being carried up a lane at midnight.

– Norman Dubie, *In the Dead of the Night*

It's late afternoon
just beginning to dark.
This is the graveyard of the day
when you think you will not move again
either forward or backward.
It is raining, slowly.
The reflections on the road
are like images washing through
a black wave.

My father-in-law drives
nervously, carefully,
as he has all his life.
He has little to say
as the car tires disappear
into these reflections
as into a play,
then reappear on the other side,
an audience clapping.

A door is opened to a house
through which pale light comes
like that from the wings of moths.
A man has entered the house,
has just come home from factory,
stockyards.
He carries a black lunchbox
into which he put the final tones
of his afternoon.

He loves his children who leap toward him
through the shaft of light.
He loves his wife standing with white dishes
like wafers of love in her hands.
His shoulders are damp with rain.
In this ceremony he has left the door open
so the other lives that pursue him
may come or go as they wish.

from

DARK LIGHTS THE TIGER'S TAIL

(1981)

IN THE OLD SEASON

He is out in the woods alone.
It's five in the afternoon,
time to huddle for tea
and dusky conversation.

All day he has spent doing thoughtless things
for spring and for the spirit.
The sun warmed him as if he were a log
with ice in his throat.

When he hears the first tree whisper
he gathers his heavy coat around him.
He looks many times into
the darkness coming toward his left shoulder.

The old season is waiting there,
short of touching him by only a finger.
If he moves fast enough now
his watery tracks will not show
in the new falling snow.

FATALITY

The curve of the road offers us
the dead from the night before.

Not having made it from field to field
the jackrabbit is a ghost on the gravel.
As I drive by he seems to raise his head
as if distracted by our conversation.
Then he puts it down like the flap on an envelope.

The next day I pass him again.
He is flatter now
and his ears have stretched like stockings.
In fact, I can clearly see
that his ears now travel
all the way up our neighbor's driveway
and disappear into his barn.

INSOMNIA

Darkness shreds a corduroy sleeve.
Children sleep. Bats go crazy
in the chimney, screeching, sounding out
their perimeter of soot.

I stay awake long into
the electric night,
watch as lightning plays its harp
across the south.

The kitten intones his private sleep,
and the hole of silence
waits for my hand.

from

WHEN I LOOKED BACK YOU WERE GONE

(1992)

THE NEW LANGUAGE

I cannot say how amazed I am to think of you so far away.
I wake up this morning and know you are in Asia,
your plane set down on foreign tarmac with you
peering from a small window.

Two days ago you were here in your old childhood bed,
your head turned to the blue Minnesota sky.
This morning you are gone, tinkling new silver coins in your pockets.
You are farther away from me who was your belly-money
than you have ever been before.

I remember when you began your long stroke away,
the cheek of the pond that winter day smooth and cold.
It seemed you were born knowing life was an icicle
that had to be sucked down to its sharpest point
before it disappeared entirely under the melt of tongue.

You were the child who would not stay put,
who was chased down again and again
through neighbor's backyards and across busy intersections.
When you were three you followed the high school marching band
down the street and back into their gymnasium.
More than once you rode home it the back seat of a squad car,
your tricycle propped up beside you.
I scolded and spanked but it did no good.

You have been chasing the sun.
Last night you crossed six thousand miles of water wilderness

with no mother to guide you.
The light of the east appeared, hovered on the ocean's rim.
Today you begin the breath-strokes of Chinese,
a pause and then the soft black line that guides you into speech.

It seemed I only turned away for one second.
A silver pencil of plane lifted you into the physics of wind and wing.
When I looked back you were gone.

DIVORCE

In my dream I could not
get the poem to fit the page.
This is the way sometimes
I do not know who we are.

Today in the late light
I saw how tires of cars
made trapezoids in the snow,
the lines cut perfectly as if
to frame a diminishing face.

And tonight my son would not go
with his father, did not want to see
the sweat and pull of young men wrestling.
Instead, he sat by me for a while,
then went to play Dungeons and Dragons,
a better world where people do not marry or divorce,
where there is no sex,
no failing.

TIME

I call the hospital room in Iowa where my children's
      grandmother answers with a shaken voice.
Here in Minneapolis it is raining.
If we were outside standing in the rain and crying no one would
      know.

I call this woman I have known for a quarter of a century
and whom I love even though I am no longer married to her son.
Phone wires spin as she grieves old age, the failing body, the
      briefness of a day.

When the sun comes out it's over twenty five years of water,
my two daughters paddling there on a slow afternoon.
She's behind us on a blanket with sandwiches, grape juice
      and towels she will wrap around us.

It is summer. Flowers drink this rain we're having. Then they
      lean, heavy, blooming, toward the earth.

MY FATHER'S LAST GAME

Today your old golf clubs arrived
with your ghost at my front door.
The date of the last game you ever played
was stamped in red on the ticket tied to the strap.
I saw how you must have hoisted the bag
over your shoulder, setting out tired
and by then not loving it much.
The ticket says: *18 holes, South Pine Creek Park.*
It warns: *Always keep in sight.*
And: *Good only on the date issued.*

My son finds in a pocket a Band-aid
kept for blisters, and a ripped black driving glove,
such very small things.
But nothing could protect you by then,
the truth of sun in your eyes,
the trees staggering farther away
as you stepped off the green.

What kind of day was it?
I want to think a white gauze day,
a few birds, you out there,
and the ball going where you wanted it to go.
My son says he has never see a sand wedge,
studies it, rubs the chip marks.
He knows this is the club for difficult places,
for the ball that will elude you
slipping down between grains of sand.

CROCUS

One crocus is in bloom suddenly.
I find it on the shelf beside
my bed with the sprawled sheets
and the empty clothes breathless
on the floor.
This flower of resurrection
forced through the hard soil
to come stabbing into air.
It is purple and gloved
like one hand folded over another
covering the secret night birth,
the quick breaths.

Now it is here,
first flower of spring
and how easy it is to wait
for the rest, accepting
the shortness of this life
which is persistent,
to be counted on,
like the sun that comes this morning
filtered through white curtains
that separate, but only slightly,
what is in the body
and what is not.

THE UNREAD BOOK

It comes toward you when you least suspect it / you are on a busy street in a foreign country and no one is smiling / and you are unsure of the language and the clouds are grey and from every direction / mothers push children in strollers who are all crying because they are hungry or bored or sad / and you step into a bookshop because it has finally just begun to rain very lightly / and you see the unread book you gave your mother the Christmas before she died / and you walk over / and you crack its spine.

AT THE VIETNAM MEMORIAL

for Caroline Marshall

We look for names.
In the yellow pages of the dead
we thumb through.
Drizzle, cold, a numb day.

I do not find my names,
the men who disappeared
from my life,
Darryl. Fred. Tom. Michael.
This means they are still out there,
married, fathers,
gone to jobs,
to padded bars at night.
I check two times to make sure.

You find your name,
someone from high school.
Boyfriend? The tallest center
on the basketball team?
Look how he still stampedes
down the court, his eyes
permanent in the glare.
The floor is slick, shiny.
And the ball released right now
from the grace of his body
goes up, over, and drops
like a head through the hoop.

We move down the marble gravestones,
so many we cannot count,
cannot help but see
our own bodies reflected,
pushed back at us darkly,
our faces tattooed with
the names of the dead.

A TYPOLOGY OF *SAD*

It's *sad* to be alive in this world where oil-soaked otters are fished from the icy waters off Alaska.

And it must be *sad* to be the wildlife specialist who has to identify the limp, black carcasses. Even I who have only a small screen TV can tell how awful it is and that someone should pay, but not money.

It's *sad* there isn't a penance, that the guilty don't have to walk in bare feet over the rocks like Irish pilgrims at Lough Derg, which is also called Purgatory. The rocks tear their skin and mark the ground with blood, extracting an atonement.

It's *sad* those sinners won't spend fifteen days fasting and then be closed in a cave so the real demons can come. On the sixteenth morning they would fall on their knees before the oil-soaked bodies.

It's *sad* this will not happen. The dead ones roll over in an oily sea, one eye to the sun, one to the dark below.

ANTIGONE IN ARMAGH,
NORTHERN IRELAND, 1984

for Bernard and Mary Laughlin

At night we cross the border,
pass through no-man's land,
a lonely strip abandoned to crickets
and the persistence of hard-luck sheep.

We're stopped at the sentry post, blinded
by a sudden yellow spotlight.
Inside the concrete bunker
a young, angry soldier from Liverpool
or the London slums checks
our license plate on his computer.
He signals us to enter.
We never see him.
We do see the spikes
embedded in the road
that will with a flick of his wrist
sink into tires of more suspicious cars.

In Armagh,
city of twin hills with twin cathedrals
that growl across the dense valley air,
we hear Antigone pledge once again
to honor her brother's death.
Driving home through the misty Irish countryside
rain moves in.
Thatches and roses fly by us.
It is easy to believe we are safe
inside this innocent non-political car.
As safe as the sheep wandering
back and forth across the border,
sheep with the red kiss
of owners on their fleece
tearing the impartial grass.

RAISING LAMBS

for Ron and Ann Gower

The lambs push their honey lips into the grass.
Each one wears a dangly red earring
that tells us shots have been given,
balls castrated,
that the long arm of ownership
has clamped its staple.
They are so small against the spring,
three of them clustered
on a field of green baize
like card players who care more
for companionship than the win or loss.
Black soft noses,
sooty legs lost in grass.
These are the no-name sheep,
wethers going in a mud-scented June evening
toward their short plump existence.

We move into the house and have lamb for dinner.
Succulent, smeared with mint and garlic,
rainbows of juice in the pockets of our cheeks.
What a fine testimony to this grass, this earth,
to these nursery-rhyme loves who will never know
how we have each wished under a full summer moon
to fall on all fours and tear the grass,
to lap water from a cold stone trough,
and to live frivolous all through one summer
before marching full-blooded, red-hearted into fall
toward the butcher's swing of steel,
his unfailing arms that take hold and love us
until we know none of it anymore.

from

BOOK OF FIRE

(2011)

FIRE SONG

The universe has no edge
and no center.
Your DNA unraveled would reach
from here to the moon.
We are vulnerable to such beauty.
In the chaos of too much,
the arranging and rearranging of tables, chairs,
the all-night cremation fires smolder
separating atoms formed in the stars
that sparked into space and time.

What do grackles find in dead grass?
They gather, then fly away together
to a roof painted the color of flame.
Rustle and breath of fire.
Our Lady of Grackles.
Pilgrimage of seed and wing.
Oh, unnecessary skin!
The red-gold tulips are somnolent
in a cold March dusk.

Earlier, I had dug and dug,
found those bright green eyes already here.
What goes into the crucible is released,
a bolt of lightning on skin,
heat between my thighs,
hot on my forehead, my arms.
On the bed our sweat mingled when I was on fire.
I'd spend the whole day humming the fire song,
tongue licking an ancient alphabet
of love and desire.

Soon moon, or no moon.
Bone dark, black arms of cottonwood tree.
Only feather of candle
and the woman with wings standing
in the doorway.

PERSEPHONE'S RETURN

Where has she been, that girl?
                    Back from her winter travels
with him
            Prince of Darkness
                    outlaw

How could she not love him?
        runic smile
                    muscled leather vest

and when she arched her leg
            like a question mark
                    over the saddle-seat behind him,
                        encircled his sweat with her
swan arms,

they exploded   spacecraft,
                    booster rocket
                        falling away as they tore into deep
space.

But today,
        lilacs.

She's back with us.
Mother's Day.   Demeter
                    out in the garden looking in spite of her
                        flowery dress
            bent and old.

What is it that propels the girl toward dark?

And the man who held her

He wants   He wants.

A single bird swoops low over the river
      where the Crime Scene van
            is parked beside a cop car.

They are down in the reeds and muck
      of the riverbank
            looking for clues.

A body.

Demeter can tell them.

            There has been a crime here.

PERSEPHONE IN HADES

It's a girl's job to go
        to Hades.

How he'd wake her in the dark
        his winter need
flesh on flesh for warmth

The dog came every morning
stood by their bed
        a trinity of heads
                birth, death and in-between
      ears   petals   paws
                  gone   now   coming

The girl reached
        the dog bowed   said the girl was holy
            a visitor from another kingdom

said it was she who must lift up
        every spring
            and lay the winter dark down

Without her only
        oblivion

Said she must give thanks for all of it:

        honey-cakes for the god
           a bone for the   bitch-dog
               her dry dugs   slippery tongue.

It begins as length of light   sun ascending

Days   like the uncoiling rose
            from winter sleep

And she
       for so long
            was nothing

a breath of bubbled air
       world enticing love
            tree budding bareness
branch to shoulder to elbow

Each morning she
anticipated
            the opening
a ladder of stars

now, now, now, now, now

PERSEPHONE AT THE SPA

She strips down to a sheet,
everything   white except fleshy
    putti cherubs on the painted ceiling.

A smocked woman says:
        you are dry, dry
old skin needing to be sloughed,
    needing exfoliation, hot oil,
        abrasion,
then the anointing of creams.

Like volcanic magma rises,
    the skin of summer bronze lifts,
        scraped off to reveal
            one layer and then another.

Sediment, fossilized sandstone,
    your face a monument to the wear
        of love and sex and grief.

And then the burning after
    the burning of summer,
        your mother's hot breath.

You prepare for him again,
    moist cotton patches
        sucking light
            over startled eyes.

The esthiologist says:
        hydrate, hydrate,
applies Ylang ylang,
        love aphrodisiac
for the wedding,
    the winter dark.

VIRGINITY

The man in the dark wool Speedo
touched between her legs as he lifted
her onto the dock at Candlewood Lake.
Her father swimming with her never guessed.
And she stayed silent.

*

Riding bareback she was the wishbone
on the fulcrum of her horse,
his spine a flyway over belly and heart,
a span of breaths and then
years and years of longing.

LIFE UNDERWATER

She swims the Y pool with her mother
dead years now. They look down
through new no-fog goggles,
a black stripe demarcating the lane.

The man on the left torpedoes by
with big black flippers.
He knows human feet are not sufficient
in this world.
On the other side, a pregnant
half-moon bellied woman laps
at good speed.
She is swimming for two,
the baby suspended in water
inside a body suspended in water.

In this world everything is clear, simple.
The body does not struggle
to stay upright.
There is no wind
and everything stays the same.
Or nearly so.

WRITING IN BED

I sleep in my mother's coffin.
I just can't leave her alone.
I don't want to see what
she looks like now.
Or even then,
that March day at the Bridgeport funeral home
as my children and I stood in the silence
and I put my hand out to open the coffin lid
for one last look against her explicit directions:
No visitation. No open coffin.
I don't want anyone looking at me
when I'm dead.

I could not,
would not do it,
not after leaving her dead in the ICU,
after the nurse turned the beeping off
and said to wait while she cleaned her up,
take out the useless tubes
so we could say goodbye.
But my brother and I said *no, no*
and the two of us held hands and ran away
through the white halls out the door
into the spring sun
We had sat with her for days,
watching as she traveled further and further
into her coma until she was no longer
there. And at the very end, my brother
held her head and said: *Some believe*
you can feel a soul leave through the top
of the head but I hung fast to her feet
as if to hold her back.

No, I could not disobey her after that.
So she went unseen into the ground,
down to the narrow space between cement walls
in her Pendleton suit worn for the first time
about which she said:
If I gain just one pound,
it will never fit.

THE LABYRINTH AT EPIPHANY

It is solved by walking
                    – St. Augustine of Hippo

for Amy

1.

What story is buried inside the snaky
mounds of the labyrinth?

Tonight, grass glistens with frost.
And the fallen leaves from the old maple tree
that have collected in this winding path
whisper into their dry, thin hands.

My wool clogs leave prints on the snowy path.
By the statue of Mary
I find a squirrel-chewed pill bottle.
It says, *Traditional Chinese Medicine: Headache Ease.*
Someone has draped Mary
with a rosary of turquoise beads.

My mind is very busy today,
ricocheting.

Then I stop, suddenly
and for no reason,
take a long breath.
The snow continues.
I can hear it.
And the four a.m. dog of my life
clicks his nails across my heart.

2.

Every time it is the same.
I step onto the path and begin to think
         I am going somewhere.

There is a destination
as in any journey.
But I go in
only to come back out
         the same way
except it is always different.
I swear
         I've never been here before.

Today I have company,
another pilgrim on the path.
We are like two horses each pulling
         a cart of accumulations:
                  memories of children
                  torn ticket stubs
                  strands of our dead hair
                  the time we fell back on the grass
                  and loved the sun.

When we meet
         she is going one way,
I, another.   We each step
         from the center of the path to pass,
a veil of blue air between us.

We are constant wanderers
hurtling through time and space.

I move toward the six-petaled center.
It is Epiphany.

Crows gather in the cold oak trees.
Underfoot, leaf mash and smudge of snow
still bearing
        the memory of all the others.

3.

Today I trudge uphill
although the ground is perfectly flat.
Just when I think I'm done
there's one more revolution,
one more initiation.

Men working nearby pack up lunchboxes,
move hooded and gloved to cars.
January dusk encroaches.

This is when we must love everything brown,
dun, umber, bracken,
bone and frozen earth.

What was it that squirrel wanted
as he sat on his haunches,
stretched his paws toward me?
Who dressed the Arbor Vitae
in their little burlap coats?

Even in this time of deep silence
everything gives itself to us
over and over.
The sere forsythia branches
against a stone wall.
The pair of mallards swimming
in their small pool of water
encircled by relentless ice.

Snow in the labyrinth.
On the path the wet indent of paws
and human boots.

There is only one way in.
Only one way out.

THE BAKER'S APPRENTICE

Beyond a glass divider
the girl with red hands is stirring
a bowl of dough.

She has on the vestments of baking,
white jacket and pants, dark net over
coal-black curls.

Her bear-paw hand holds a jar of peanut butter.
She spoons it into the bowl
along with a splash of vanilla.

The old wooden spoon begins the circle dance.

Tonight more snow and again the next day.
Now the oats go pouring in,
make a fist of stickiness.

Then it's all scooped out, dollops
on the greased baking pan, tiny breasts,
low hills of sweetness.

Late afternoon dusk approaches.
The city's homeless look for a night's shelter.
And some of us admit we do not know much.

The doughy kisses wait for the oven,
sit obligingly with no fuss.
Soon she will pull down the drawbridge of heat,
slide the pan in,
close the metal door behind them.

DRIVING THE OLD KASOTA ROAD
ON SPRING EQUINOX

Down the black river road,
water a necklace around tree trunks,
straw matted on pale ground.
The doe is crumpled from the night before,
folding back even now into dead grass.

Balance, when the wolves are equidistant,
when all things hug the center,
I am both held and let go,
both melancholy and filled with love.
My life pools in dark water
beside fence posts on this night journey.

From the west a boat of darkness
pushes against dropped sky,
black against blue.
I look for you, look to tell you.
I forgive.
I am forgiven.

NEW POEMS

(2018)

I

It was the last nostalgia: that (s)he should understand.

Wallace Stevens

OPENING

Even though I can get the lawn mower going
with one hard pull
everything is still harder to open –
my friend's small packet of horseradish
that accompanies her half sandwich and soup.
Jars of pineapple salsa.
And my mouth?
Oh, no. That opens happily,
gaily, the pink cavern
missing only some words.

But back to opening the show,
curtain going up.
Everything is harder now,
muted like pale lilies
that will not toil or spin
but only gaze the daylong summer
from rapture to rupture to eruption.

So open it again, darling,
throw up the shade, lean out.
Everything has prepared you for this.
Open the gate, the door, the latch,
open your very own eyes.
The tall dark iris is incredibly speechful.
And the incessant dawn birds
will not stop talking to the sky.
Blood moves through love and tissue
and the lilacs come mons veneris,
come again all purple, sweet.

FAIRY TALES

I never believed Rumplestiltskin,
that he could weave all that straw into gold
no matter what the story said.
Or that the slipper would fit Cinderella.
Or that Hansel and Gretel would escape the oven.

I've tried the bread crumb trail.
It doesn't work. The crumbs scatter.
Or something eats them.
Or I forget where it was
I wanted to return.

But I did believe in prayer,
a child's hands folded in a flesh steeple,
a cathedral of bone and vein.
And I believed in faith.
No fairy story.
No magic at the end.

Just the dark sacrament of Requiem Mass.
And the pause in the priest's recessional,
standing under a steeple bell to sprinkle
holy water down my mother's coffin
before she was carried out into sun.

BEAUTY IS NOT ENOUGH

after Edna St. Vincent Millay

Or love. Or courage in the face
of spring come again.
The toothless woman at the intersection.
Old men on the corner
out with their cups for coins.
Where did they come from?
Where do they all go?

In the ground then.
My mother died in spring
The crocus was just coming blue.
The beard of snow around her trees
was shrinking, going into earth near the rock
where she had my father, before he died,
kill the snakes that lived there.

It is not hard to grieve.
You simply put your hands to your mouth
and scream.

LEAVING: CLEAVING

Hydrangea blossoms on the lawn where a woman
wears a big pink cancer hat   the sky

blessing us   with a confection of truth:
but clouds are not white   not breath and mallow

but a liquid family   marched
against   don't try

to follow   to make sense
of cancer   of a woman's head picked bald

what the neighbors did to starving girls
who let German officers   feed them

their heads shaved   the town square
a sky like this one   blue, a few clouds

a frequency from   far away
to have someone else's   life

the window's blue   mouth
there is no scream you can't hear   lilac scream

scream of holes   the fabric of years
a doppler of clouds   like the woman who told me

of losing her hair   one strand at a time
on her pillow   her clothes   her shoulders

in the shower   each strand a falling through
a thought of leaving   and cleaving.

SETTING THE ACUPUNCTURE NEEDLES

for Pat Cosello

My acupuncturist leans
toward meridians, toward
the practice of *chi.*
There is a light hiding under my skin.
She will open the pinpricks of doors.

In the Gross Anatomy Lab
acupuncture students practiced
on cadavers, donated bodies
with no need any longer
for the aqua chenille sweater,
the baggy legs of trousers.
Their bodies were drained of all last meals
and the throbbing circuits of blood,
drained of all autobiography.

Today her needles bite, no more than that.
I do not really feel them,
like I do not feel *exuberant earth*
or the *void brightening.*
I just feel hard love,
needles in my forehead, earlobes,
crown of my head,
a hundred convergences.
I am light rising.
I do not bleed.

THE BOX

I loved the shape of it
square with a soft
pink cover
and that pinkness
was an invitation
to kiss, to sit and lick the mucilage
which is what I did
until the box folded back
into an opened love letter
an aerogram to the world
dark and swarming.

THERE IS ALWAYS ENOUGH DARK,

and enough late summer sun for the hibiscus
                    to splay open her petals

with sweet purple and raise
                    her erect stamen,

another blossom smaller, redder
                    at the tip of her orange spike.

What is she thinking
                    that old girl?

Here I am!

            Here!

                    Now!

LISTENING FOR SINATRA

When an irresistible force such as you
meets an old immovable object like me

– Cole Porter

When the car bumped my hip as I rode
a yellow bike down the San Diego street
it could not have touched me more gently –
a Lexus white sedan that just kept on going.

I've not been kissed in a long time, especially not there.
Was this some angel on her eternal mission?
Where was it she was supposed to go?
Who was to be picked up for delivery?

She must have stopped, looked down at her GPS,
drifted slightly into the bike lane
between the car and me.
But I was not her assignment.

I only teetered, not toppled,
wobbled like a bright striped toy,
the car door and silver lock
reflecting my amazed face.

Now there are four splotches
of bruise on my hip from
the invisible driver,
the wind, the very air
kissing, kissing.

GUARDIAN ANGEL

She's the one assigned to you personally at birth,
like a security code or your own admin assistant,
the one who goes everywhere you go and never
sleeps through your sleeping.

When you run bloody from your house in the dark
she hovers over the hedges and stop signs.
She never fails you, never gives up at
the pace of your disorder.

She's there when you get drunk on Jim Beam,
throw up. When you push your husband
through the glass door, she's
on the other side waiting to catch him,
to sweep up all the broken light.

Now you both are tired,
she from watching,
you from her nervy affliction.
She's an old angel
like a used car,
a dark green Chevy Nova
up on blocks in your driveway.

Your poor guardian with her smoky exhaust,
tears in vinyl seats,
and a windshield cracked
by flying rock into
the starry kaleidoscope
through which she still watches
the hole of your back.

THE CELLS—THE MOON

after Kiki Smith

Amoeba, lacy jellyfish, doilies,
or buttons on her good going-to-church coat.
Knobs on a radio, a mandala.

The moon rattled inside her frequently.
When she puts out the wash on a thin line.
And when he comes home, drops his tool bag
by the front door, clicks on the TV.

The moon is a place apart
beyond rapping at the kitchen window.

The timer on the microwave simpers pale yellow.
And she is a kimono of possibilities:
breasts, legs, rib cage,
sarcophagus, bells,
balls of twine.

She says *I can't remember the last ten years*
puts her head inside the necklace,
her ribs an extra set of corset stays,
the corset an extra set of ribs.

Which one was taken from the man?
Which one does he want back?

NOAH'S WIFE

In the Boundary Waters, we ran out of cigarettes.
My husband tried smoking leaves,
fir needles, moss, anything that could be burned
but it was no good. We saw no one.
Only stars: Ursa Minor, Cassiopeia.

Weeks we portaged through swamps,
neither land nor water,
carrying food, sleeping bags, tent.
We drank rain, fried fish he caught.
On the last day a moose swam toward us
and my husband, scared, yelled
paddle, paddle faster, get away!

Our first night on solid land he drank
a whole pint of brandy,
danced naked around our fire
at the landing where black bears came down,
pawed the dented dumpsters.
It was Christian Brothers brandy,
not wine that he drank
before he finally passed out
and I could plunge into my dream of the moose
swimming fast toward our canoe,
his antlered head a candelabra above cold waters
carrying light into the world.

ECTOPLASM

The news today all bad.
News of endings.
Of death, of sickness.
Of sickness unto death.

Then three/quarter moon
in the east, rising.

My old life reaches out with
tentacles and tentacles.
Well-meaning,
but tentacles, nonetheless.

What is memory if not
that grey octopus,
ectoplasm?

Please don't go.

II.

Why do we think history is full of stops and starts?
The future is only the past turned around to look at itself

Fanny Howe

DEMETER SPEAKS

1.

She wants to get
married. I haven't even
met the guy. Or
his family. She's only
a high school sophomore,
didn't go to the volleyball
tryouts because she felt *ill*.
That girl loved volleyball,
the push-pull over the net,
the little red shorts. I say *wait*
until after college. She says
no to waiting.

I tell her if you get
married you can no
longer call this home.
She says *that's ridiculous*.
I say *have sex*
all you want but don't
tie the knot. It's a legal
contract. If he buys a bright red
Mustang and can't make
the payments
they'll come after you.

She says *If I have a baby,*
it will look like you.

2.

Hades was the one
to show up with the tent camper
and the old dog,
just the two of them.
They were both looking into the woods
and for what?
For me, she said.

She petted his dog.
There was a green fleece blanket
with an antlered stag.
He had a small red cooler.
She sat and drank an RC with him
at the scarred picnic table.
She says he was in recovery.
Or he's divorced.
Or he reminded her of her father.
He wore a blaze orange hunter's cap
and had planted a small flag
by his campsite, C23.

He sat there all afternoon
waiting for her.
And me?
It was like cutting off
my arm.

THREE HOUSES DOWN

A girl died yesterday.
The EMT cradled her in his arms,
laid her on the stretcher outside.
She was a husk, an empty cocoon.

Heart arrhythmia,
as if the heart could play only one song.
There were kids at the house
running around, shouting.

I was up on my stepladder
painting my old red fence one more time
before winter.
Women gathered in her front yard,
brought food, stories.

All night they continued to come
and the kids ran and yelled
and the stories were like wasps,
like flies at the screen door.

Later I fell asleep to crickets,
heard sobbing, a voice
outside my window under the linden tree
saying it over and over:

I don't know what to do.
I don't know what to do.

EVERY MISSING GIRL IS PERSEPHONE

In memory of Anarae Schunk, 1994–2014

The eye doctor dilates my eyes.
Black holes swell, let in all the light.
That's why when we find a body
we check the pupils,
shine a sharp light,
wait for the opening up.

Your body is in the reeds of Lilydale
down by the river,
your pupils closed,
the light gone out.
We searched for you,
girl who loved the bright narcissus,
your white dress knife-cut,
the sky is so blue today nothing can be hidden.

The ophthalmologist tells me I have healthy eyes,
says I'm good for two more years
and although I can't see clearly,
I walk down three flights of stairs,
exit into the dazzle of parking lot,
get behind the wheel of my car.

The world is still beautiful to see
as if for the first time.
Do you remember it,
those first moments in the light,
blazed, dazed, shocked,
and you all new and shining again,
taking it all in?

PENELOPE

Better to have re-
venge.
Better to not
wait.

I got old
waiting,
scaled skin,
old plum between
my legs
and two ripe
avocado breasts.

I never wanted
to be Penelope,
tearing out all
I had woven
warp and woof together
every damn night.

My suitors were
a blanket of gnats.
When they slept
I unraveled
what I pretended,
wove instead
all the women
from the seasons
of rage:
at war, at home,
bodies found
beside a dirt road,
the one buried in a freezer chest,
the one in the river,
the ones still missing.

READING FRANK O'HARA

Oh, Frank! I wish you were
still here. It could be
1958, you in NYC,
me, only sixteen, just up the road
in Connecticut frequenting
overgrown Revolutionary War graves
with my Brownie camera.
We could have been friends.
There'd be so many things to say.
You'd tell me not to be
afraid of my life.
You'd tell me it's okay
to move out of my parents' house
and live at the YWCA.
You'd say *don't bother with*
the shitty girls on the synchronized
swimming team. Go for the
race team, burst your heart
like your mother worried you would,
swim the marathon
across Long Island Sound
from Port Jefferson to
Black Rock Harbor.
Be your fishy self.
At the Y on Golden Hill Street
I swam freestyle
up and down twenty,
thirty, forty, fifty laps.
I was built for endurance.
Oh Frank, we could
have shared a lane.

OCEAN BEACH

The way each wave takes its own place to break
and roll toward shore in a half-moon of white water

and the way the man is tossed off his paddle board
with each wave and gets back on

the same way the bird came right down into traffic on the I-5
this morning, a suicide bird tornadoed off the hood of a car

like the way the boy who only wanted adoration
killed himself   but not the way the carp

adored me as they thought of fish food
all of us swimming in one mind the way silver melts

the way the pelicans follow grief
and the way I only want to hold on

waiting for the sun to burn a hole in the sky
and for the way the sky shuts the red down.

AFTER FIRST FROST

the vision comes,
trees bare
sun high, far away
earth tipping
as I tip all night
under the Biederlak blanket
that was my mother's,
that she gave me,
or that I took after she died.
Either way, her DNA is still on it.
That never dies.

I've heard when new doctors
graduate from Harvard Medical School
they receive a gift of
Grey's Anatomy
bound in human skin.

I don't think this is true.

PENELOPE, AGAIN

It's never over for the bees
or the small songbirds that befriend your garden.
Even your very own skin doesn't know
what errors you've made,
what mistakes in judgment,
taking or not taking someone to love.

Your dog rises to go to the gate,
barks away anyone passing.
The yew is winter brown.
Still you bend your head to spring,
open windows, throw wide the door
of your life, try to find the one
who went missing so long ago.
Are you finally ready for love?

Clear the burn of December and January,
those angry sisters.
Clean out the wren house.
Next door the boys are trying
to start their car.
The horror of combustion.
These boys repeat themselves
with their stuttered song
over and over and it will not run.
But you are in the garden,
got bird, got skin, got sun.

THRESHOLD

This is not a poem but a silence
even though there's noise,

news with the latest disasters.
This is not a poem but a facsimile

like the mannequins in stores.
You think someone's there but

she's not seeing you even though
she looks your way.

Sometimes it seems like
I've come back from the dead.

That I've been gone but now
reemerge and I know that can't

be true but I feel it the way a curtain
undulates back and forth and I step

through from one side to the other as if
it could be that easy, the coming

and going, the holding of breath
and then the breathing.

A friend's daughter is dead –
four days ago, she just stopped

breathing. Another friend is on dialysis,
passing from empty to full every other day.

Sometimes sitting in my chair,
I'm there and then I'm gone

someplace else, some other life
careening toward completion.

This is not a poem, not a drowning
not a fence to keep me out

but a linen invitation to the singing.

III.

Perhaps beauty
is the mother of death
not the other way around.
Perhaps the rain itself
is an answer.

– Linda Pastan

SHE WORRIED ABOUT HER HEART

It felt too big for her suddenly
as if it were taking over.

Some days she could hardly
keep it in her chest.

Dear heart.
Just go on,
keep beating.

She'll do her part
to make room for you,
push her ego away
like it's filler, fluff,
wet kapok.

Her ego is all head.
He does not like to take
a deep breath.

He's the step-child
who was spanked
with a hairbrush.
Having said that
she feels calmer,
feels she can go on.

REMAINS

I sprinkle the cat's ashes in the garden down among the iris,
the mint, and near the catnip.

I free the short white pieces of her bone, legs, and spine,
and the grey shale of the rest of her.

There is not much that survives a fire.
The cat went up in the smoke a year ago.

It has taken me this long to find a place to let her go.
Later, I closed the garage door for the night.

Someone said a cat was meowing
but it was only the sticky hinge.

WHAT THE BODY KNOWS

I heard a poet read about his mother's dementia and
remembered my friend telling me about his cousin's wedding,
the barn dance after, how his three older sisters
who all have Alzheimer's danced all night,
remembering by heart the two-step,
the polka, the schottische,
and I remembered my mother in the ICU that last time,
how she pushed off her blanket in front of the doctors,
challenged them to look at her trim ankles,
and her legs that carried three full wombs,
legs that bumped from stove to dumbwaiter,
legs that carried our laundry to the roof to hang,
legs that swayed to Guy Lombardo and his Royal Canadians,
Ritz Ballroom, New Year's Eve, 1940,
those legs, defying God and death and the doctors,
legs that remembered *Enjoy Yourself,*
Auld Lang Syne, and
I Want to be Happy.
Those legs,
that dancing.

LANDING PLANES

We are where we're not supposed to be.
We're supposed to be on the ground,
terra firma, not up here, inside this bird-shaped fuselage.

Outside only emptiness and thin air.

Minutes ago our plane had dropped down
ten thousand, eight thousand, four, then city, cars, lights,
over the river, over the interstate,
almost touching.

The jet's tires hit the runway hard,
not a kiss but a smack – bang, bang.
For seconds we seemed to float.
Then the plane accelerated and we,
incredibly, rose up again.

An albatross airborne, captive.
One wing tips, then the other,
We head into red sun, everyone silent
except kids peering down at a shrinking world.
Outside, cloud. Inside, pure possibility.
It was time to remember other planes,
other passengers.
The man beside me closed his eyes.

Then we bank left, down again,
descent a slow devolution that we
believe or don't believe.
We touch earth.
The Wizard says:
Pay no attention
to that man behind the curtain.

THE BIRDS OF QUINTANA ROO

She doesn't know what day it is
nor do the birds of Isla Mujeres.
They yodel all morning and all night
with voices rubbed like palm fronds.
Black catbird with a scissored tail,
poor will, nightjar, flycatcher jay,
bandy-legged. All fly away from her,
but not the squeaking fan,
not the dove.

In her next life she'll learn
to speak properly
the language of birds.
In her next life
she'll have forever
although that clearly isn't true,
not as true as the Gulf of Mexico,
or as true as her heart
turning azure, sea-glass blue.
Her hair is electric.
Her thighs and elbows spark.
The clouds don't dare her.

She won't put her glasses on.
She will write, will see blurry
the small insect on her chair,
the man up the beach in the red shirt.
She's in the next life already,
crossed over the threshold,
all the birds guttering
and the paddle-tailed black bird,
a clarinetto, swimming.

LAST BLESSING

Merida, Mexico

My mother would have liked it here.
Men wear gold crosses under white linen shirts.
The women are bright in their huipils and rebozos.
At night white-flowered carriages appear
pulled by small horses. Yesterday,
I saw a man cradle his horse's hoof
looking for the stone, the irritation.
Day of the Dead skeletons wear trays of beer on their heads.
The Virgin, the Wise Men, and Joseph row a boat shaped
like Sirena who protects them from drowning.

Today there is rain on the pigeons and the portals,
rain on those waiting at the Cathedral of San Ildefonso,
sheltered under the great arch. When the priest stopped
my mother's casket as it rolled down the aisle
of the Church of the Assumption of Mary,
stopped it with his censer and holy water,
I loved her as she lay under the nave, under the bell tower.
And when the bells began the priest flung out the last blessing,
gave his hand and his condolences to my brother,
but not to me and my unbaptized children, her grandchildren.

Now the rain is letting up. My mother never saw this church,
built over a Mayan pyramid by Mayan slaves
with stones from their own destroyed temple.
Here the jaguar god protects children who travel
between the worlds at night. And, the great snake
still sits on goddess's head, hinging and unhinging
the open maw of her jaw.

ISLA MUJERES

On Isla Mujeres one is advised to watch the water,
to drink from the coconut,
to tattoo the serpent down your thigh.
The sky is a slash of pink blood-water.
The 13th sin is not seeing small lights in dawn houses.
A blush of sun from one side, moon on the other.
Then blue door blue table blue pool of blue water.
The birds are blue. My white bed is blue.

At La Tienda de Abarrotes the baker pauses,
hair-netted, gowned and gloved.
He leaves the massaging of dough to bag the buñuelo
I have placed with silver tongs on a silver platter
He seals the bag and I bump and grind all the way to the cashier
on an island where the Gulf meets the Caribbean
and the goddess, Ixchel, has a serpent on her head
and not smashed under her feet.

I have frigate birds in my hair.
It is hard to anguish in island weather.
I wear silver into the sea, into the rain,
tokens, shiny lures for shark face and barracuda fang.
Iguanas prowl over rocks inside stillness.
I don't see them. Then I do.
How close things become in the rain
as if we were not separated
by birth at all. The singing birds.
And the cats.

Mongrels prowl the beach.
Clouds don't come any closer.
Nobody seems to be in charge of
my ascent or descent.
Then I realize I've gotten over it,
finally.

CAPTIVA

A wrist of new moon over Captiva.
Palms rattle their blades.

The Gulf sways in relief of the night
with its star explosions,

its manic music-making.
And if you begin again

it is because you have been asleep
in the curve of the earth,

one foot in this world
one in the other

wherever that is,
where the palm blades turn,

where there are drumming
creatures in the high sea grass

and conch shells that look like gladiators' helmets,
gastropods, bivalves, two halves of everything

sand in all its molecules,
the heft of wild rose and morning glory

wind pushing shells up from dark,
each one a thought, an idea

of flesh and bone
and the wind down the sound alley

explodes in the heart over and over
ospreys and cormorants,

the sea bird that stretches her wings out
facing the sky like an angel and then

perches so still in the mangrove tree you
hardly see her but you do see

the genuflection, the open gown of Mary
Saint Francis taught us to honor

and the overweight woman who arrives
for a cold swim as the sun sets

swimming up the pathway into the sun
no matter her thighs, the swinging flesh of her arms,

the water where she is weightless
airborne as she swims right up into the sky.

SPEED OF STONE

From the place where I am I've already left
                    – Manoel de Barros

I look back the long road.
No gas pump.
No general store.
It's sage & sand
& love of asphalt
lying across the hurt.

In the dream I bought silver ear hoops,
quick like a rabbit. Or a coyote.
A fix. All fast
and no longer present.

Manoel, I saw your shadow
on the page of my book
where it says:

      From here all I glimpse is the border
      of the sky.

The lines danced.
Perhaps it was an illusion.
Saint Theresa's face on a dishtowel.
The Virgin on a wall of mud.

JACARANDA, SAN DIEGO

Flowering jacaranda on every block,
a bridal veil of purple purpose casting
iridescence at your feet only to astound you
like your father in 1943 here on his way to war
and you a baby home in the cold east-coast apartment
with a mother afraid of snakes and lightning,
a mother who cleaved to shadows,
shade-drawn black windows.

Here under the jacaranda your whole past melts away.
Gone the soft stinging from what was not love
but a facsimile of love or a like-love,
unlike the jacaranda that could be taken for all your life
just now in this place with no purpose but to feather the ground
each thought a petal off the blooming branch
so you can have it flowering blue
through all your crossing over.

NOW

after the art installation by Susan Boecher

Now you've made a blanket, a rug of curls
On the floor of the gallery, remains of your hair
Worked like buffalo hide, the hair a

Necessity thrown down
Over the chemotherapy cliff
Where cancer flooded. You did

Not always see it go
Onto rocks below, the
Wreck, the damaged skin.

Nets fell like pollen, oat grass
On your shoulders, your pillow
Wept a rain that would not stop.

Nights in your shower left
Oblique lines on white tiles,
Writing like scribbles because cancer does

Not make any sense. It's some
Other language, gibberish
We don't know, language we

Never want to know
Or ever translate, the
Whisper, grammar of fallen hair.

Now I want to lie down
On the rug of your hair,
While your new hair grows

Newly honeyed against you,
Open to air, brushing your face as you
Walk all the way to the river and back.

WANTING TO DO SOMETHING FINAL

About dying and then
just not caring anymore.

How would death sound
in another language?

More beautiful, melodic?
Je suis mort. Estoy muerto

The robin is throating her good night
sundown song from the old blasted tree.

She faces west, can see it there,
gold shield disk of one eye closing.

Still she sings on. What can we do
with all our loving?

What can we do with all
our skies and grass and hot burning?

What to do finally with all
these questions?

GOING UP LOOKOUT MOUNTAIN

Grateful for legs that can sleep on the ground
and still rise up the next morning,
that can squat to pee and rise from squatting
though it is difficult.

Grateful for sky over Lake Superior,
for this day, though it is fall and soon winter.
Grateful for fall, for the dying away
though I know only some of that,
the anxious heart, the blood pounding.

Grateful that among dead and fallen birch
someone has encircled seedling pines
inside little wire cages against the deer.

Grateful nothing else is as black
as the shriveled fruit of the Amanita mushroom.
Grateful, too, for the deadly Amanita,
Destroying Angel with its bowl of pleasure.

Grateful to cross the Cascade River at the falls
on my way up the mountain and meet
the wedding party, Persephone in white,
carrying crimson mums, her eyes smoky
with kohl and her gown folding
over her like wings.

Grateful for all of us here, mother of the bride, father,
the others waiting for the minister to show up,
the boy ring bearer who climbs the split log fence
that keeps us from cascading down
into the rush of white water.

Grateful because I can hear it now,
that roaring.

SEPTEMBER GOLD

A host of sparrows at the safflower seed.
        Across the alley, my neighbors burn
old window frames. Cardinals appear.
        The sun moves to light up my arm.
It's September, finally. Too soon for regret.
        Where have the lovers gone?
My body is tired. And I've missed
        something important.
Orpheus loses Eurydice by turning.
        Don't look back a poet says.
Underground isn't the place for that.

* * *

On Rosh Hashanah, a white slice of new moon
        like a ram's horn.
Soon, Yom Kippur. I'm not Jewish but I want
        a day of atonement.
What do I remember from my dream?
        Who shall live and who shall die?
After ten days of repentance
        I might pass in the air before God.

* * *

I think I'll find the way.
        I sit on my language suitcase, unpack words,
ligatures drawn in space.
        We are all going like Moses to the Mount.
I will love myself with all my heart,
        will take no false selves before me.
I will not steal.
        I will not covet another life.

THE FIRST TRUTH

Bellows of lungs. Air sacs.
Balloons flying high.
Who holds our string?
Or do we just go kiting away?

I've been angry.
I swore at other drivers.
I swore at myself,
at my own stupidity.
And at the stupidness of things,
things that went left when they should go right,
things that dropped, that fell,
that came unscrewed
or that wouldn't unscrew at all.

I just want to say
(as if it wasn't me)
Go on putting
one foot in front of the other
along the road to the volcano
where something ends – land
and something new begins –

Oh, star of fire!

ACKNOWLEDGMENTS

I owe a debt of gratitude to so many who have supported me over the past fifty years and to whom these poems are dedicated:

To Robert Bly for his mentoring and his friendship that was so important to a young poet;

To Harvey Gross who introduced me to contemporary poetry at the University of Denver;

To my publishers: Robert Bly (again), Ron Wallace, Tony Oldknow, Jim Perlman, and especially, Norton Stillman;

To Roseann Lloyd in appreciation for her fine editorial eye;

To Kate Green, favorite traveling and writing partner;

To Cass Dalglish for her unwavering friendship;

To the wonderful friends and fellow writers I have met along the way: Margaret Hasse, Mary Kay Rummel, Sharon Schmielarz, Ethna McKiernan, Carol Connelly, Kate Dayton, Pat Barone, Kate Kysar, Kris Bigalk, Lynette Reini-Grandell, John Minczeski, Mike Finley, Greg Watson, Louis Jenkins, John Rezmerski, Doug Green, Sean Thomas Dougherty, Matt Rasmussen, Patrick Werle, Matt Mauch, Donte Collins, Kirstin Bratt, Vicki Keck, Carol Masters, Candyce Clayton, Jim Lenfestey, Margaret Rozga, Tim Nolan, and Athena Kildegaard;

To my much missed Dear Heart, Phebe Hanson;

To my colleagues at Augsburg University, especially Kathy Swanson who hired me to teach creative writing. And to the MFA Program, especially Stephan, Lindsay and Kathleen for their good humor and patience;

To my students at Augsburg who have taught me so much about generosity and kindness. Thank you for your open hearts;

To Partricia Canelake for sharing the cover painting;

And to my family—Amy, Bridgit and Devin—who keep me together. And my grandchildren—Izzy, Aaron, Winona, Marshall and Graham—who are the best companions I know.

NOTES

The title "There is Always Enough Dark" is from a poem by W.S. Merwin.

The title "Beauty is Not Enough" is from a poem by Edna St. Vincent Millay.

"The Cells—The Moon" is after a bronze sculpture by Kiki Smith.

Cary Waterman is the author of six books of poems, including *The Salamander Migration* from the University of Pittsburgh Press and *When I Looked Back You Were Gone* from Holy Cow! Press, a finalist for the Minnesota Book Award. *Book of Fire* from Nodin Press was a finalist for the Midwest Book Award.

Her poems are included in the anthologies *Poets Against the War, To Sing Along the Way: Minnesota Women Poets from Pre-Territorial Days to the Present,* and *Where One Song Ends, Another Begins: 150 Years of Minnesota Poetry.* Her poems have been awarded prizes in the Federico Garcia Lorca Poetry Contest, the Rash Awards, the *Common Ground Review* Poetry Contest and *So To Speak*, the feminist journal from George Mason University.

Her memoir, *Horizon*, appears in the anthology, *The Heart of All That Is: Reflections on Home*. She has also published reviews and essays widely and was co-editor, with Jim Moore, of *Minnesota Writes: Poetry* published by Milkweed Editions.

Cary has received fellowships from the Bush Foundation, the Minnesota State Arts Board, The Loft, and the McKnight Foundation, and has had residencies at the MacDowell Colony and at the Tyrone Guthrie Centre in Ireland. She received the Loft-McKnight Award of Distinction in Poetry.

She has taught at many colleges and universities, most recently in the MFA Program at Augsburg University. She lives in St. Paul.